Dust Bowl Survivors

Patti Trimble

Contents

Rigby®

A Harcourt Achieve Imprint

www.Rigby.com
1-800-531-5015

"You Couldn't See a Thing"

On April 14, 1935, families on the Great Plains in the south central United States watched the sky grow darker at the horizon, even though it was too early for nightfall. They noticed a looming cloud of dust, hundreds of feet high, blowing toward them across the prairie. The air thickened as it filled with dust, and the huge cloud began to block out the sun, quickly turning the sky as black as night. This frightening afternoon became known as "Black Sunday," but the storm was only one of hundreds that swept across the Great Plains in the **Dust Bowl** of the 1930s.

During the Dust Bowl **era,** crops failed, livestock died, and farmers and businessmen went broke. Life on the plains became so difficult that hundreds of thousands of families decided to abandon their ruined farms and start new lives in other places. Many stayed on, but they found it almost impossible to make a living on the dry, windblown land. The Dust Bowl marked a time when people on the Great Plains had to struggle every day just to stay alive. For the survivors, it was one of the worst experiences in memory.

Black Sunday represented the worst of hundreds of dust storms to hit the southern Great Plains in the 1930s.

Dry Farming on the Plains

The Great Plains were once covered in acres of wild prairie grass, and they stretched out like golden blankets as far as the eye could see. The rich soil of the plains made it ideal for farming, but until the late 1800s, this wild prairie had never been **cultivated.** The Comanches and other Native American tribes had once lived on these plains as **nomads,** moving from place to place, raising horses, hunting buffalo, and gathering roots and other wild plants. Their presence slowed the settlement of the plains by farmers, but once the Native American hunters had moved on, the vast prairies of the central United States were opened up to new inhabitants.

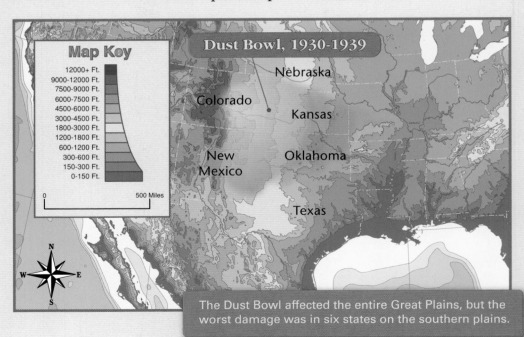

Dust Bowl, 1930-1939

Map Key

	12000+ Ft.
	9000-12000 Ft.
	7500-9000 Ft.
	6000-7500 Ft.
	4500-6000 Ft.
	3000-4500 Ft.
	1800-3000 Ft.
	1200-1800 Ft.
	600-1200 Ft.
	300-600 Ft.
	150-300 Ft.
	0-150 Ft.

0   500 Miles

Nebraska

Colorado

Kansas

New Mexico

Oklahoma

Texas

N W E S

The Dust Bowl affected the entire Great Plains, but the worst damage was in six states on the southern plains.

By the late 1880s, much of the West was viewed as unoccupied land that needed to be settled, so the United States government thought the best way to move people into those areas was to advertise in other countries to encourage people to **immigrate.** The government wanted to make sure that these **immigrants** would settle in the West, so it offered free land to families who would set up homes and farms there. Many of the new immigrants who came to the United States had little money and no farmland, and they were eager to begin new lives in America.

Farmers and other workers already living in the eastern U.S. saw the promise of free land on the plains as a chance to improve the lives of their families. They quit their jobs, sold their homes and businesses, bought wagons and teams of mules, and prepared to move out onto the prairie.

Beginning in the 1880s, thousands of people moved onto the Great Plains to begin farming the land.

Thousands of families packed up everything they owned and headed west, joining the rush for land ownership. When a family arrived in Oklahoma or Texas, they searched for a piece of land that no one lived on and filed a claim with the U.S. government. Families built houses out of whatever materials were available and began farming the land, a process called **homesteading.** Once a family had homesteaded, the government sent them the official **deed** to the land.

Because lumber, brick, and stone were scarce, some farmers built houses out of sod, or cut blocks of dirt and grass.

Farmers grew grains to feed cows and horses, as well as vegetables to eat and to sell at the market.

Most immigrants and many of the eastern farmers expected life to be better out on the plains, but they learned that this wasn't necessarily the case. The soil on the plains had never been broken by a plow, so it had to be loosened sufficiently for crops to be planted. The first farmers had only lightweight plows pulled by horses or mules, so the farmers could only prepare small sections of land at a time.

The Great Plains also received only 20–25 inches of rainfall a year, which was less than other farming regions received and less than most crops needed in order to grow. Farmers had to adopt the practice of *dry farming*. They dug deep wells to reach natural underground stores of water called **aquifers.** Wind-powered pumps drew water to the surface, and the water was used to irrigate crops. Farmers also dug huge pits, called tanks, in their fields to hold water for crops and animals.

Although the work was hard, early farmers in the West managed to make a better living than they had in their home countries. They were happy to have a one- or two-room house, a couple of horses or mules to plow the fields, one or two cows to milk, and a few chickens to lay eggs.

Most families grew enough vegetables to feed themselves during the summer and had plenty left over to store for the winter months. They also grew extra crops so they could sell or trade them for other things that they needed, like cloth for making clothes, fuel to heat and light their homes, and flour for baking.

By the 1920s, more and more farmers had moved onto the Great Plains. They adapted to the requirements of dry farming, but their other farming methods came from their experiences in the East or from their home countries.

At first, most farmers on the Great Plains were successful. The rich soil produced plentiful crops.

Soil erosion can occur when there are no plant roots to hold the soil in place.

Most studies of farming methods had also taken place in the eastern states, where soil and climate conditions were very different. In the East, farmers and farming experts had never been greatly concerned with the possibility of **erosion,** the wearing away of soil by wind or water. But soil erosion posed a particular challenge in the West, where strong winds were common and sudden downpours could wash away dry soil quickly.

9

One man who recognized the problem was Hugh Hammond Bennett, a soil scientist working for the U.S. government. He realized that the roots of trees and other plants, including grasses and crops, held the rich **topsoil** in place and prevented it from being eroded. He began to warn farmers about the dangers of leaving the soil unprotected.

Hugh Hammond Bennett warned American farmers about the dangers of soil erosion.

Erosion can destroy a farmer's fields. The destruction can prevent the raising of crops for years afterwards.

However, there were almost no trees on the Great Plains. The prairie grasses had done a good job holding the rich plains topsoil in place for thousands of years, but as more and more farmers began to plow more acres of land, the soil was exposed to the forces of erosion.

The development of the steam-powered tractor seemed like a great benefit to plains farmers. Tractors could plow more than 5 times the number of acres in a day that a team of mules or horses could plow. But tractors meant that even more soil was exposed to erosion.

Then two events happened at almost the same time that spelled disaster for thousands of residents of the Great Plains.

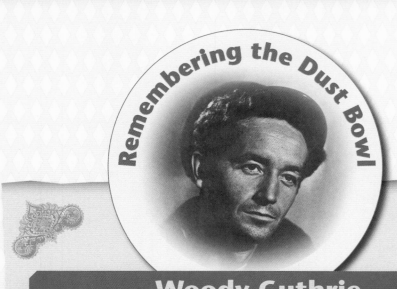

Remembering the Dust Bowl

Woody Guthrie

Woody Guthrie was born in Oklahoma in 1912 and grew up on the plains of western Texas. He and his family experienced hardships such as illnesses, house fires, and job losses, and when he was 16 years old he set out to make his own living. He turned his musical talent and the sympathy he felt for other unfortunate people into a career as a songwriter and folk musician.

Guthrie became famous for his song "This Land Is Your Land," but he also wrote many songs about the experiences of Dust Bowl survivors.

On the 14th day of April of 1935,
There struck the worst of dust storms that ever filled the sky.
You could see that dust storm comin', the cloud looked deathlike black,
And through our mighty nation, it left a dreadful track.
It covered up our fences, it covered up our barns,
It covered up our tractors in this wild and dusty storm.
We loaded our jalopies and piled our families in,
We rattled down that highway to never come back again.

Verses from Woody Guthrie's
"The Great Dust Storm"

Depression and Drought

With so many farmers planting so many more acres of crops by the 1920s, the supply of farm products rose dramatically, resulting in a drop in prices. That meant that farmers weren't paid as much money for the same size harvest. The solution seemed to be to plant even *more* acres of crops. To accomplish this task, many farmers borrowed money from banks to buy more equipment, mules, horses, tractors, and land.

In the fall of 1929, prices on the New York Stock Exchange began to drop rapidly. Banks that had invested money in stocks suddenly found that their stocks were worth less and less. In order to raise money, banks forced borrowers to pay off their loans early. Farmers who had borrowed money to pay for new land and equipment had a big problem: they would only have money to pay the banks after selling their harvested crops. Thousands of farmers suffered **foreclosure,** the loss of their homes, farmland, and equipment to the banks, because they couldn't pay back their loans immediately.

By 1929 many farmers owed money to banks for land and equipment.

14

A worker begins to clean up the floor of the New York Stock Exchange. In October 1929, stock prices fell so low that many people lost millions of dollars.

The stock market "crash" plunged the country into a money **crisis** called the **Great Depression,** which lasted for more than ten years. Banks and businesses closed, millions of people lost their jobs, and thousands of people were forced to beg for food or a place to sleep.

After foreclosure, vast acres of fields stood plowed but untended on the Great Plains. Farms were abandoned. Farmers who were able to keep their farms found it hard to sell their crops because people didn't have enough money to buy them. **Surplus** fruits, vegetables, and grain rotted in barns and warehouses.

During the Depression, jobs and money were scarce. This photograph shows people lining up for a free meal.

The drought that began in 1930 dried out farmland throughout the United States. The southern Great Plains, however, were the hardest hit.

The Depression, however, was only the beginning of the troubles. In the summer of 1930, it stopped raining. It didn't completely stop; farmers hoped that they were only experiencing a temporary dry spell, but in much of the Great Plains—especially in the southern plains states of Colorado, Nebraska, Kansas, New Mexico, Oklahoma, and Texas—rainfall dropped to about half its normal amount. Wells dried up because not enough rain fell to maintain the water level in the aquifers.

Huge expanses of plowed farmland baked in the hot sun. Without rain, not even the prairie grasses or weeds could grow back. The southern plains began to look like a desert.

For four long years, the sky remained a clear, cloudless blue. The sun beat down every day on the southern plains without letting up, causing temperatures to soar. Then beginning in 1934, the winds began to blow.

Strong winds had always swept across the plains, but the intense heat had caused the winds to grow even stronger. Coupled with the long drought, the wind acted like a giant broom, picking up the dry, powdery soil and carrying it up into the sky. These enormous, towering clouds of dirt and dust rolled for hundreds of miles across the plains.

Dust storms blasted every acre of the plains with dirt, which settled over the land like brown snow. Dust piled up on houses and barns, and it buried entire fields. The dust swelled and poured across the farmland, and farmers and their families began to get used to the fact that everything they owned would be regularly covered with a thick, new layer of dust. Since it was the 1930s, Dust Bowl residents began to refer to the time as the "Dirty Thirties."

People stopped being surprised at the sight of dust clouds gathering on the horizon. In the flattest areas, people could see the dust coming from more than thirty miles away, but there was little they could do to prepare for a storm.

How Do Dust Storms Happen?

Dust storms are common in dry, windy parts of the world, such as Africa, India, China, and parts of North and South America. Several conditions must be present to create a dust storm:

- High temperatures
- Drought or drier-than-normal weather
- Loose soil with few plant roots to hold it in place
- High winds

Sometimes people tried to escape the dust by fleeing in their cars.

Tom Lea

Tom Lea was born in El Paso, Texas in 1907. After he finished public school, Lea attended a famous art school in Chicago and studied drawing and painting. From 1926 to 1933 he taught art and worked as an illustrator in Chicago.

During the Great Depression, the U.S. government hired artists to create large, wall-sized paintings to decorate public buildings such as schools, post offices, and courthouses. Lea was one of these artists, and his paintings depicted scenes from life on the Great Plains before the Dust Bowl. They reminded people of the beauty and rich history of the region.

Lea became famous as a book and magazine illustrator in the 1940s and 1950s. His best-known pictures capture the feeling of life on the open plains.

"And There He Was" by Tom Lea

Living in the Dust Bowl

Imogene Glover was a child during the Dust Bowl era. In the late 1800s, Imogene's grandfather took his family and headed out west, following a dirt trail through Texas to settle in Oklahoma.

Imogene's grandfather, father, and older brother built the farm, working hard to make a living for their family. They constructed a small house and barn, put up **barbed wire** fences to mark the farm boundaries, and then bought farm animals and planted crops. At first they raised melons, but when those didn't sell very well, they planted their fields with wheat. Next her father decided to raise turkeys, and over the years the family was able to **prosper.**

Imogene remembered life on the plains as pleasant but lonely. Her family was happy and her parents and grandparents took good care of her, but her nearest neighbors were miles away. No one visited her family's farm very often.

Imogene remembers vividly the day the dust storms began and how her family eventually learned to live with the dust, day in and day out, for years. One day Imogene's teacher was driving to school and was caught in a dust storm, and the dense, black cloud of dust covered the road so that it completely disappeared. But looking up, her teacher realized that she could still see the tops of the telephone poles that lined the road, so she slowly guided her car by looking up at those poles, which led her straight into town and to the school!

Travelers in the dust storms often became lost or had accidents because the dust made it nearly impossible to see.

When the storms hit, the wind blew harder than it had ever blown before. Imogene Glover and her family worried that their house might blow away, sweeping them away with it, and she remembers running to hide in the cellar to escape the winds.

Sometimes, after they were safe inside, dust piled on top of the cellar door, making it impossible to open, so Imogene's father brought along an axe in case he needed to break open the door. He also brought a scoop to shovel away the dust and a long-handled rake to poke the dust out of the air vent in the ceiling.

Imogene always brought something to read, because she knew they might be sitting in the cellar for a long time, waiting for the dust storm to pass.

Melt White was also a child during the Dust Bowl years. He was just a young boy when the storms first hit, and he remembers how frightened his family was. In those days, people had few weather reports to warn them of approaching storms or even to explain what was happening, and neighbors lived too far apart to warn each other. Melt's family would notice a low, black cloud bank forming in the northwest, and they would watch it grow larger and larger as it moved closer, the edges of it sweeping around until it seemed as if the world were being swallowed by a giant beast.

"Finally it'd just close in on you, shut off all light and you couldn't see a thing. The first one or two that happened, people thought the end of the world had come. Scared 'em to death . . . they were just hysterical," Melt said.

There was almost no escaping the dust storms. The clouds of dust swept over farms quickly, with little or no warning.

Like many farm children during the Dust Bowl years, Melt White lived with his family in a small, one-room wooden house. When the dust storms hit the farm, the wind howled from every corner of the roof, and it shook the walls, windows, and door.

In the late afternoon of April 14, 1935—Black Sunday—the worst storm the White family had ever seen blew in from the northwest. Melt was in the yard helping his father hitch the family's horses to their wagon so the family could go to church. On the distant horizon, Melt and his father saw the low, dark wall of the dust cloud, and they could see it moving closer. They knew there would be no church for the family that evening.

Even people who had lived through years of drought and dust became frightened during the storm on Black Sunday.

Melt and his father put the horses away and hurried the rest of the family into the house, taking shelter from the approaching dust storm. The sky grew darker as the wind howled, and Melt remembered being afraid that the house might blow away. The walls shook and rattled, and even though it was just after 5 o'clock in the afternoon and well before sunset, the house became as dark as if it were night.

Soon it grew totally dark, both inside and outside the house. Melt tried to see his hand in front of his face. "I kept bringin' my hand up closer and closer and closer and closer, and I finally touched the end of my nose and I still couldn't see my hand. That's how black it was."

On Black Sunday, the dust was so thick that it clogged noses and throats and made it very difficult to breathe or see.

Melt's father lit a lamp and set in on a table across the room. Even though the lamp was only a few feet away, Melt could just barely see the light because there was so much dust in the air inside the house. He remembered Black Sunday as "the blackest, worst dust storm, sand storm we had durin' the whole time."

Simple wooden farmhouses and barns offered little protection from the black clouds of dirt and dust.

Dirt and sand piled like snow against farm buildings on the plains.

Imogene Glover remembers another terrible dust storm that blew up one night as she and her family slept in their two-room house. She was asleep in the small room, and her parents and baby sister were sleeping nearby in the big room of the house. Suddenly, she heard a loud crash: the storm that had started so suddenly had dumped a gigantic load of dust on the roof. The dust was so heavy that the ceiling had fallen in, and sand and wood covered her parents' bed.

Luckily her father had heard the roof creak, realized that the roof was collapsing, and woke his family so that they were able to escape in time.

Imogene remembers the dust and described it as thick and heavy, like black powder.

Dust filled the yards and the homes, swallowed up roads, and buried tools and animals that had been left in the fields. Wind blew the topsoil, dust, and sand from one end of the plains to the other. Nobody could believe the **devastation**, and still no rain came.

Dust storms arrived with surprising and frightening speed, not always giving enough warning to allow people to get to safety. Children were caught in swirls of dust as they walked home from school, and the sand burned and scratched their legs. Adults were sometimes caught in a blinding wall of dust that would cause them to become lost on their own farms. They learned to feel their way back to their houses, following the lines of the wire fences with their hands.

Even between the storms, the dust remained in the air, so a new daily chore was added to farm children's lists: cleaning out the noses of the farm animals. A layer of dust coated the inside of people's noses as well, and this made it hard to breathe. Every morning people found themselves coughing up dirt. Some children and old people suffered from a form of **pneumonia** caused by dust in the lungs. Parents were especially worried about babies and very young children, so before going to bed at night, they would place a sheet over their children to help keep some of the dust away from them.

The dust storms made more work for everyone. People had to scramble to keep their houses clean and to keep the dust out of their food. Imogene remembers her parents turning all of their plates and cups upside-down on the tables and covering them with a sheet.

Farm families tried to seal their homes against the dust by stuffing sheets and towels into cracks in doors and windows.

To most of the people who lived through the Dust Bowl, this hard, dirty life was simply another part of life on the plains, and they accepted the dust as just another hardship to endure. Children like Imogene Glover had never known any other kind of life before the dust storms, and she thought the dirt, grime, and **poverty** were normal.

In fact, Imogene thought she was one of the luckiest children because her parents took good care of her. They ate the same food for every meal—cornbread, beans, and milk—but at least they always had food on the table. Her family never went hungry.

As the drought continued, water became even more precious. Few farmers had indoor plumbing, so they got their water out of the few deep wells that hadn't dried up and stored it in barrels. Farm families often had to walk quite far to get the water, and then they had to carry the heavy water all the way back to their homes. They used that water for cooking, drinking, and watering their animals. Because water had become so scarce, Dust Bowl farmers and their families took fewer baths and washed their clothes only when absolutely necessary, even though they were almost always dusty and dirty.

Melt White remembers the layer of dirt and dust that settled on his family's drinking water every night. Each morning, he had to **strain** the water through a piece of cloth to remove the larger pieces of dirt and twigs.

Many Dust Bowl children and their parents became used to the heat, wind and dirt.

33

Melt also remembers how the government helped his family survive by giving them food, called commodities, including prunes, canned grapefruit, and mutton, the meat that comes from sheep. Sometimes they were given lard, a thick, butter-like substance made from animal fat, or spicy sausage. They felt very lucky when they got flour, which they could use to bake bread and make pancakes.

Farm families like the Glovers and the Whites were not making any money by clinging to their land. It would be years before conditions would change enough to allow farmers in the Dust Bowl to make a good living again. But the Glovers and Whites, and a number of families like them, withstood the bad times and remained on their farms.

Dust Bowl families received some food items from the government.

With no crops to sell, the farmers stayed very poor, and when the terrible dust storms showed no signs of stopping, many people decided to leave the Dust Bowl. Growers in California sent hundreds of advertisements to the Dust Bowl states, claiming that there was plenty of work in California. These advertisements promised good pay and said that thousands of workers were needed to harvest the many crops that grew in California. They claimed that a person could just help oneself to any of the food that was being picked.

The half-starved farmers imagined themselves in sunny, dust-free fields, picking peaches and eating as they picked, with their clean and happy families by their sides. California began to sound like a magical place, so the farmers sold their animals and their heavy equipment, packed up their households, and headed west with their families.

Dust Bowl familes were often poor, but most were able to keep food on the table.

Remembering the Dust Bowl

Dorothea Lange

Dorothea Lange grew up in New Jersey and went to school in New York City. After college she moved to California, where she worked as a photographer.

At the beginning of the Great Depression, she noticed all the homeless people on the streets and began to photograph them, hoping that her pictures would lead more fortunate people to try to help those who had lost their homes and jobs. U.S. government officials saw her photographs and hired her to take pictures of victims of the Dust Bowl, because the government wanted to gain support for its programs to help poor farmers.

Lange's photographs are among the most famous in American history. Her pictures can be found in books, libraries, and museums all over the country. Lange worked as a magazine photographer into the 1960s.

"Migrant Mother"
by Dorothea Lange

To Leave or to Stay

Between 1930 and 1940, more than 1 million people left their farms and homes in the Dust Bowl states and moved to California. People already living in California referred to these people as *Okies,* even though many also came from Texas, Kansas, and Colorado, as well as Missouri and Arkansas. The government called these homeless farm families **migrants.** The migrants headed to California expecting to find work in the fruit and vegetable fields, and they hoped the work would lead to better lives for their families.

Most migrants traveled west on U.S. Highway 66 (known as Route 66) through the deserts of the southwest to California. Route 66 became littered with broken-down cars and abandoned furniture and belongings during the 1930s as people tried to get to California any way they could. If a family's car or truck couldn't complete the trip, they sometimes split up and sent children ahead with friends, or occasionally even with strangers. Men and women frequently climbed aboard moving trains and rode them as far as they could, jumping off to find another train to carry them west to the dream of California.

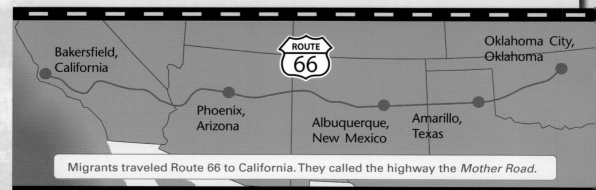

Migrants traveled Route 66 to California. They called the highway the *Mother Road.*

NEXT TIME TRY THE TRAIN
RELAX Southern Pacific

Dust Bowl migrants made their way to California any way they could.

When the migrants first reached California, the green fields and valleys seemed to match the paradise they had dreamed about on their long journey. Stretched out as far as they could see were miles and miles of fertile, irrigated fields and orchards. But the hopes of many were ended before they could even settle into what they thought was their new home.

Most adult Dust Bowl migrants had little or no education, and not all migrant children had gone to school regularly. They sometimes found it difficult to get information about jobs, food, or places to live.

Often the poverty of the migrants meant that they did not have shoes or even spoons to eat with. Constantly walking barefoot, eating with their hands, and infrequent baths meant that many migrant children suffered from diseases.

Migrants soon began to see signs along the road telling them to keep moving, that there was no work. They were told that all the jobs had been filled. People shouted at them from the sides of the road to go back home. Growers in California sometimes refused to give surplus crops to hungry migrant children, hoping that the parents would go back where they came from. The word *Okie* was soon turned into a bitter insult.

A few people turned around and went home, despite the fact that their homes in the Dust Bowl had become a wasteland. More people, however, chose to stay in California. As the Great Depression dragged on, many found temporary homes in government camps. Most migrants had used the last of their money for gasoline, and now they had reached the end of the line. They had no work, no food for their families, no place to go, and no way to get there. They had left a harsh, poor life in the Dust Bowl for a new life that was in many ways even harsher and poorer.

Many of the migrants began to wonder whether they might have been better off staying back home in the Dust Bowl rather than chasing the dream of a better life. Some, like the Glovers and Whites, had stayed home, but it was difficult to say which was the better choice.

Some workers arrived in California after abandoning their homes and farms in the Dust Bowl, only to find that there was no work to be had.

Farmhouses on the Great Plains were far apart, and farm families had very few neighbors, relatives, or close friends. The loneliness increased as more and more people left for California. Like those who had left, many who stayed wondered if they had made a good decision.

Imogene Glover's father never lost hope that his own luck would change, and even with the piles of dirt and dust and the long hours of work, he was careful never to act disappointed with his life. After each bad year and failed harvest, he believed the rain would come

Often, the farmers who chose to stay in the Dust Bowl were the most hopeful — or the poorest. The work never got easier, and it was years before their farms began to be successful again.

soon and that the next year would surely bring a big crop and a chance to make good money. He thought that if anyone could make it, he could.

Melt White believed that his father stayed for another reason: the family simply wasn't able to leave. The Whites owned no car and had very little money. They owned a wagon, a plow, two horses, some kitchen goods, and the clothes on their backs. They weren't going anywhere.

John Steinbeck

John Steinbeck grew up in Salinas, California. He attended Stanford University and lived briefly in New York City, but he returned to California to write books.

When the Great Depression and Dust Bowl disasters started, Steinbeck was angered by the bad treatment and terrible working and living conditions of the people who had come to California to escape the drought and dust on the plains. He worked to try to improve the lives of Dust Bowl victims and other poor farm workers, and he wrote his most famous book about them.

The Grapes of Wrath tells the story of a family of Oklahoma farmers who lose their land to foreclosure and are forced to look for work picking vegetables in California. The book won many awards and was made into a movie. For a great number people today, what they know about the Dust Bowl comes from Steinbeck's book.

Steinbeck won the Nobel Prize, the highest award a writer can receive, in 1962.

THE
GRAPES of WRATH
John Steinbeck

The cover of John Steinbeck's
1939 book

The U.S. government helped the families that stayed in the Dust Bowl region to borrow money so they could keep their farms and gave out surplus food from other farming areas. Government officials visited the farms and bought sick and starving livestock that couldn't be sold, paying the grateful farmers $10 to $25 for each animal. Families were generally glad to receive help from the government after their animals and crops were gone, and believing that their farms might not be saved, the farmers began to take any jobs they could find.

In 1936 Melt White's father earned $25 to appear in a U.S. government film—this was nearly two months' wages for only a few hours of work! The film showed how the farmers' plows had ruined the plains, how they had caused the erosion that led to the Dust Bowl, and how farmers could protect the soil in the future.

Melt and his family were given free tickets to the film's opening night—the first movie they had ever seen. Melt remembers sitting in the theater with his family and finding it hard to believe that his father was beside him in the theater and also plowing the fields on the big screen.

In 1935 the U.S. government declared that soil erosion was "a national **menace**," and Hugh Hammond Bennett was named head of a new government department called the Soil Conservation Service.

The SCS programs taught farmers how to keep the topsoil in place and new ways to plow and plant. The government paid farmers to follow these new methods.

Hugh Hammond Bennett worked to teach new and better ways of farming on the plains.

In 1937 farmers began planting trees supplied by the government across the Great Plains, in clusters stretching from Canada to northern Texas. Farmers were paid to plant cedar and ash trees, varieties that grew naturally in the region, and to take care of them.

Farmers learned not to leave fields unplanted; they seeded their empty fields with sunflower seeds provided by the government. The sunflowers helped hold the soil and provided food for wildlife.

Farmers also learned to plow their fields across the direction that the wind tended to blow. This helped stop the topsoil from being carried away.

Hugh Hammond Bennett knew that the roots of trees hold soil, so he started a tree-planting program.

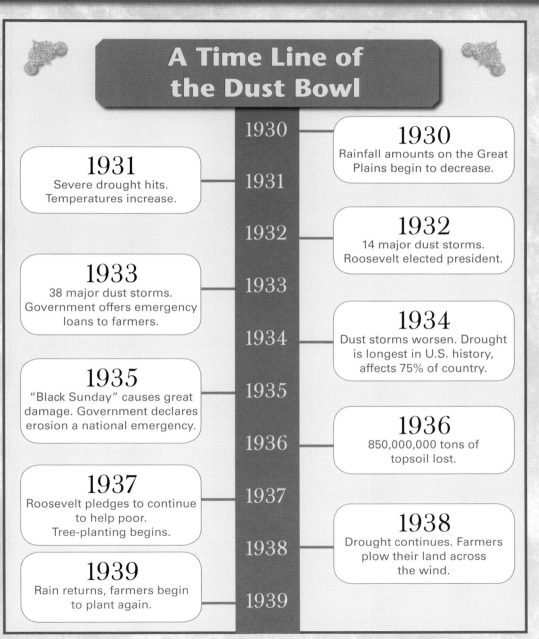

A Time Line of the Dust Bowl

1930
Rainfall amounts on the Great Plains begin to decrease.

1931
Severe drought hits. Temperatures increase.

1932
14 major dust storms. Roosevelt elected president.

1933
38 major dust storms. Government offers emergency loans to farmers.

1934
Dust storms worsen. Drought is longest in U.S. history, affects 75% of country.

1935
"Black Sunday" causes great damage. Government declares erosion a national emergency.

1936
850,000,000 tons of topsoil lost.

1937
Roosevelt pledges to continue to help poor. Tree-planting begins.

1938
Drought continues. Farmers plow their land across the wind.

1939
Rain returns, farmers begin to plant again.

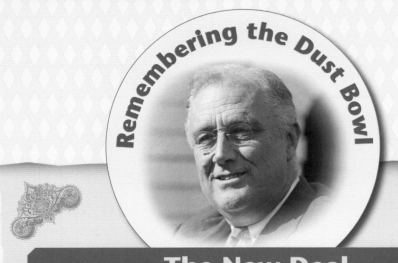

Remembering the Dust Bowl

The New Deal

When President Franklin D. Roosevelt took office in 1933, the Great Depression had been going on for more than 3 years. Millions of people were jobless. Dust Bowl farmers and others were losing their homes and land because of falling crop prices and foreclosures.

President Roosevelt immediately asked for new government programs to put jobless people to work and to help save homes and family farms. Roosevelt called these programs his "new deal for the American people," and the name stuck.

One New Deal program paid farmers *not* to plant certain crops in order to reduce the supply of farm products, so prices would go up. Another program hired farmers to work for regular paychecks on land owned by the government.

Many people criticized New Deal efforts as expensive and wasteful. But most people believed that the New Deal helped relieve much of the suffering of both the Dust Bowl and the Depression.

A poster for one of the New Deal
programs created to help farmers

Rain!

Then in 1939 it finally began to rain again, and the dry land began to change. Once again the damp topsoil stayed in place, seeds sprouted, and crops grew. As farmers resumed plowing, planting, and caring for their fields, they knew that things were getting better; each year, less and less soil blew away in the wind.

Sadly, thousands of people had been left in poverty because of the Great Depression and the Dust Bowl, and the families that returned from California had to start all over. Many found themselves living in government camps again until they could rebuild their homes, farms, and lives.

Many people never returned to life on the farm. Men and women in increasing numbers began to seek jobs in cities, and farms were sold to neighbors or to large farming companies.

Those who survived the Dust Bowl will always remember the dust storms that they lived through and the hard times that came with the storms. Families like the Whites and Glovers still live and farm on the Great Plains today; they will never forget how hard they struggled to stay alive on this land. They hope, like all plains farmers, that they have learned the lessons necessary to avoid another Dust Bowl.

Dust Bowl farmers welcomed the return of awesome Great Plains thunderstorms. The rain helped to restore their damaged fields.

Visitors to the Great Plains now can see fields of grain, cotton, soybeans, and even sunflowers. They are irrigated by rain and by water from deep wells.

Today farmers across the plains work hard to prevent soil erosion, and they watch wind and weather patterns carefully in order to be prepared for difficult times. They know drought is a constant threat, and only through careful planning and the use of scientific farming methods will another Dust Bowl disaster be avoided.

Scientific farming methods and careful planning have meant a return to success for Great Plains farmers.

Glossary

aquifers natural underground water supplies

barbed wire wire with sharp, pointed pieces; used for fencing animals

crisis serious problem or trouble

cultivated prepared for growing crops

deed written contract for a piece of land

devastation severe damage or destruction

Dust Bowl area of the southern Great Plains hit by severe drought and dust storms in the 1930s

era period of time often lasting several years

erosion wearing away, ususally by water or wind

foreclosure taking back property because of lack of payment

Great Depression 10-year period of worldwide money problems beginning in October 1929

homesteading settling and farming on previously unsettled land

immigrants people who move into a new country

immigrate to enter a new country

menace threat or danger

migrants people who move from place to place within a country

nomads people who live by following the animals they herd or hunt

pneumonia serious disease of the lungs

poverty having little or no money or goods

prosper succeed

strain clean by pouring through a cloth or screen

surplus extra; unsold

topsoil fertile, upper part of the soil

Index